ONE KING'S MISSION

"CONCEIVED IN CONSCIOUSNESS, BORN TO THE REVOLUTION, RAISED AS HOPE"

BY,

KING MISSION

Cover, cover art, and interior design by:

www.lulu.com

Photo taken by King Mission

Back cover art:

King Mission

ISBN: 978-1-105-64548-8

ONE KING'S MISSION

"CONCEIVED IN CONSCIOUSNESS, BORN TO THE REVOLUTION, RAISED AS HOPE"

BY,

KING MISSION

Dedicated to my parents who showed me that the crown a King wears is made up of his character…not his claims.

TABLE OF CONTENTS

INTRODUCTION

"Many Choose and Few are Chosen"

--The Almighty Latin King and Queen Nation

The decision to join the Almighty Latin King and Queen Nation is one that not only changes the life of the individual joining, but also has an effect on the lives of those who are close to the individual. I made the decision to join at the tender age of 15, with the complete support of my parents. Through the years, I have had many opportunities to learn from others in the Nation, teach others in the Nation, affect positive change in the Nation, and ultimately gain a greater understanding of the community as a whole by gaining a greater understanding of the dynamics that exist within the Nation.

The following pages are comprised of sentiments that I have shared with my royal brothers and sisters. I share them with you now in the hopes that you can gain a greater understanding of One King's Mission.

ALKQN QUOTES

1. The Nation is more than literature, meetings and rules; The Nation is a lifestyle full of personal relationship.

2. Many want to wear the crown, but few are willing, prepared, and passionate about building the crown.

3. My throne exists on the souls of my community's feet. Each and every day I sit and prepare myself to be trampled by those who are my social and cultural reflections. While others view this as a punishment, I view this as an honor; For when the Almighty Father calls me to stand, I do so inevitably raising my community.

4. From the moment I was exposed to this tangible life, I was a Latin King. From the moment the Almighty decided to warm me with the light of our Royal brotherhood, I was the Almighty Latin King Queen Nation.

5. We are lions with our own unique language. To the untrained ear, our words are heard as simple roars. However, to those who stand in the light of the Almighty Father, our roars are heard and understood as expressions of brotherly and sisterly love, honor, obedience, sacrifice, and righteousness; as well as growls of respect, honesty, unity, knowledge, and love.

6. Though we strive for peace, may we always find the strength to keep our swords sharp and our shields shiny.

7. It started with Love and has found eternal life through Love.

8. My crown is in my heart and in my mind; it will never be taken off of my existence, as an article of clothing, and put to the side.

9. My willingness to die for my brothers and sisters is made royal by my commitment to live for my brothers and sisters.

10. We should learn from the past, not get stuck in it.

ARE YOU GANGSTER?

Amor de Rey y Corona, familia. As always and forever, I hope that when you read these words you and all in your Kingdoms are in the best of health and spirit.

Today, I find myself pondering the concept of how it is that we identify ourselves. I wonder what term would best describe us… both internally and externally. I review the comments on all of the unauthorized websites that exist. I read the profiles of those who call themselves Kings and yet act as clowns. I look at the public pictures of those who call themselves Queens and yet present themselves as whores. I study the sentiments of those young brothers and sisters who say they are the future, but then show no value of human life. I lose myself in all of this and more and wonder, "What word best describes us?" I wonder if the word we use would be the same as the word that the community would use.

With these questions bouncing threw my mind, one stood out… "Are we gangsters?" This question made itself more personal and more manageable and so I pose it to all of you; "Are YOU a gangster?"

Ask yourself….

When you walk down the street, do you do so with aspirations of the community bowing down to you?

Is every step you take dripping with the desire that you be recognized as the biggest and the badest?

Do you want those who oppose your way of thinking to be inspired by fear at the mere mention of your name?

Are your actions to be understood differently because you are you?

Do you pray for your name to "ring bells" on the streets of communities all over the world?

When you sit to eat, do you fill yourself with a plate full of fame and wash it down with an ice cold glass of envy?

Do you brag that your title is that of a killer?

Do you laugh when others hide from you?

Do you justify your lack of personal progression by claiming that the streets needed you 24 hours a day and days a week?

If you have answered yes to any of the above questions, then I ask you… Why do you hide behind the name of the Almighty Latin King and Queen Nation? Why do you thrive on damaging the name of a Nation that means so much too so many? Don't you feel shame in mocking the Almighty Father, King of Kings by claiming to be one of His children, and yet not abiding by the rules of His house?

When I walk down the street, I do so lost in thought on what it is that I can do to improve my community. I do not want anyone to bow their heads, for our communication is most affective when we our eyes meet. Those who are honored are my elders who have already contributed their youth to the struggle and now deserve to be cared for and listened to… not pushed aside and left to die.

Each and every step I take, I do so as an instrument of the Father and a tool of the cause. I alone have accomplished nothing and the biggest there is, is the Father Himself. As for being regarded as the baddest; I have no desire to join the ranks of my oppressor.

If my name is to inspire anything, let it inspire a sense of brotherhood and love. Let those who hear it, whether they agree with my personal views or not, understand at the core of their existence that I love my community and dedicate myself to its upliftment. Let it be known that I am a mortal and have no dominion over any other mortal. The Almighty Father has blessed us with the gift of free will, and with that gift we have made the decision to join and abide by the rules of the Almighty Latin King and Queen Nation. Fear? No. I want those who oppose my thinking to be inspired by Love. Not love of me, but love of the community as a whole.

As well as being subject to the rules and regulations of our beloved Nation, I am also subject to the civil rules of my community. My existence in the ALKQN does not entitle me to any special or preferential treatment.

I do not pray that my name ring any kind of bells, for the only music I yearn to hear is the music that is created when our voices are united and truly stand together.

When I sit and eat, I do so first ensuring that all of my brothers and sisters have already eaten and obtained nourishment. The menu consists of selflessness and anonymity. I do not crave fame and do not thirst because of envy. The legacy that I work towards is not about me, but about the progression of all of my brothers and sisters.

The only title that needs to be mentioned is that of "King" and the only position that inspires me is that of "Brother".

There is no humor in those who I exist to serve hiding from me. If the members of my community do hide from me, then their action does not demonstrate fear… but rather, it exemplifies their intelligence as they see that if I am not following the guidance given to me by the Almighty Father.

If I do not strive to obtain and maintain personal progress, then I do not fully believe in the cause of the ALKQN.

So again, we are back where we started. Now tell me…. Are you a gangster? Or are you a King / Queen of the Almighty Latin King and Queen Nation?

Let me ask it differently… Are you a child of the Almighty Father, King of Kings, who He has selected to serve His other children and improve their communities? Or are you one of His children who has betrayed Him and in thinking yourself greater than all others, served as the authors of turmoil and despair in our communities?

Many want to wear the crown…. But few are willing, able, and passionate about building it… and even less are devoted to understanding it.

Are you still thinking? Are you unsure?

I invite you to stand in the light of our creator and with the absence of all that is unrighteous ask yourself; what are you?

BLOODLINE VS. KMC

Amor de Rey y Corona, familia. As always and forever, I hope that when you read these words you and all in your Kingdoms are in the best of health and spirit. As for me, I continue to draw from the Brown Force of my Ancestors as well as the guidance of the Orishas to maintain my Kingdom.

Family, the issue that is addressed in the message written by Brother Ambition below, is one of great concern to me. The alleged war between what is known as Bloodline and the KM/C is nothing more than a plague fueled by ignorance that leaves communities burned with confusion and division.

While many have come to have passionate opinions regarding this "debate", few have actually existed long enough in the formal Nation to know the truth and facts about the history and the origin of this debate. What is probably the most ironic fact is that the individual who first formally introduced the term "Bloodline lessons" is not even a member of the Nation anymore.

Brothers and Sisters, the misconception that the teachings of our Brother, King Blood, inspire separation between the family needs to be eliminated. The belief that Brother Blood had dreams of taking over the entire Nation is a belief kept alive by the hyenas in our Nation that enjoy dressing up as Lions and attempting to roar. THERE IS NO TRUTH BEHIND IT!!

On a consistent basis, Brother Blood directed the family to learn, understand, follow, and uphold the teachings of the motherland. These directives came both verbally and in written format.

To charge a piece of paper with being the cause of one's death or downfall is to ignore the lifestyle that the person who passed away lived. Documents do not breathe life into our Nation… The blood, sweat, and tears of living brothers and sisters does! We must cure ourselves of the disease that strips our children of a future… we must cure ourselves from the ailment that ensures our demise… we know the name of our enemies… They are called IGNORANCE and LAZINESS.

THE TRUTH AND THE FACTS NOT ONLY EXIST, BUT THEY EXIST FREELY. THEY ARE NOT OWNED BY ANY ONE BROTHER OR SISTER. INSTEAD, THEY ARE OWNED BY EVERY BROTHER AND SISTER!!

I have been given the opportunity by the pioneers of this website, to inform you all that division of any kind will not be tolerated on www.alkqn.org. While we are all encouraged to express and share our opinions, feelings, and ideas, the line between expressing one's opinion and disrespecting the opinion of another, will not be crossed… the line between expressing a feeling and disregarding the feelings of another, will not be crossed… the line between sharing an idea and giving an order, will not be crossed.

For those of you who cannot see passed the areas, tribes, and/or chapters that claim to "run a certain way", I invite you to communicate with those brothers/sisters. Perhaps there is more to their standpoint than meets the eye. Or perhaps, they are truly resting comfortably in the shade caused by division and primitive thinking.

I regard myself as a Nation man… I take each and every sentiment that is either spoken or written by a true child of the Almighty, as royal guidance. I do not hear them with speculation that they are trying to take over the world. I understand that as the world changes, the manner in which we rule must change. I challenge all in my family to do the same.

We cannot start a breath embracing all who say they represent the crown, and then end that breath damning those whose stones shine differently. The fact is that every beam of light that hits our crowns comes from the Father. And every stone that adorns or crown has been inspired by the imperial design dreamed of in the motherland.

All text that has enabled to us to move forward in our commitment to empower our community was first uttered y the Almighty Father and planted as an idea into our heads by Him… have we strayed so far away from the light that we think we are better than it? Have we perfected our own individual lives so much, that we now have the right to pass judgment and speculation on the lives of those who are regarded a brother?

Plain and simple… there is nothing in the lessons referred to as Bloodline that opposes the teachings of the King's Manifesto Constitution. There is no mistake that the King's Manifesto Constitution is our foundation… we build on it.

CONSPIRING AGAINST KING'S LOVE

Amor de Rey y Amor de Corona, Familia. As always and forever, I hope that when you read these words you and all in your Kingdoms are in the best of health and spirit. As for me and mine, we continue to draw from the Brown Force of our Ancestors as well as the guidance of the Orishas to keep our heads up. Family, I come to you concerned about an issue that has plagued our Nation almost from day one; but with the luxuries of modern technology, has come to plague our Nation today in ways that should be truly unimaginable.

The issue I am speaking of is the one that presents itself when brothers and sisters of our precious Nation use the terms: "Brother", "Sister", "Nation", "Amor de Rey", and "Amor de Corona", as empty sayings to mask their hypocrisy, jealousy, and desire to conspire against their own for their own personal selfish gains. Perhaps I should define what I consider to be "conspiring against", as it is probably the most "sensitive" of the allegations that I am making above…

How many of us know of that "secret meeting" that was

supposed to take place between half of the tribe? How many of us have heard that brother/sister who has all the answers for how things should be done, but still can't follow them himself/herself refer to other members of our precious Black and Gold family in a negative light behind their backs? How many of us have seen brothers/sisters smile in the face of their Nation Kin as long as they were getting something they wanted/needed, only to hear them express their dissatisfaction with whatever it is they got? How many brothers/sisters have we caught in a lie that defined their inconsistent character? How many of us have witnessed brothers/sisters throw their life away for the sake of the "Nation", while talking negatively about those who offered them nothing but selfless love and assistance while they got "back on track"?

Unfortunately, if we were in a room raising hands, more than half of them would be up. In my opinion the above questions represent both conspiring against and preparing to conspire against, our very own Black and Gold brothers and sisters.

You see, when our body is divided, it is weakened. Those who claim to have the answers of how we can improve our conditions and uplift our Nation as a whole should not have to express themselves in secret with lies attempting to cover their tracks. Those who are truly chosen by the Almighty Father to wear a crown should not have to refer to their brothers/sisters with contempt. When a meeting is secretly called to discuss the dissatisfaction that one or two members of the body may have, but the source of their alleged dissatisfaction is not invited or present, then the meeting loses all validity. Why, at that point it should not even be referred to as a meeting. It would more appropriately be regarded as a whining session, where alleged Kings/Queens take their crowns off and complain about those absent with no real desire to fix anything.

Unfortunately, these events are usually orchestrated by one character that as we used to say it back home, "Puts the batteries in everyone else's back". This one individual is usually one who has benefited in every possible way by the very force that they are complaining about, and is simply looking for the way to make himself/herself popular. They long for a name in world that they feel has treated them unfairly or that simply does not understand them.

The end result of the events mentioned before is seeds of distrust, disgust, animosity, and misunderstanding being planted into all parts of the Lion. This animal that is supposed to represent the royalty of our precious Nation then becomes ill and eventually dies. Every conversation has a negative undertone, every comment a side meaning; at the end of the day, how can you respect or acknowledge one who has allowed words common to the vocabulary of our enemies to spill from their mouth, as a brother/sister? When we allow our time to be filled with thoughts and conversations of "what if's" that end with a sincere member of the body not being around ("What if brother A wasn't around us anymore?", "What is we did our own thing and did not tell Brother B?"), then we allow ourselves to be guilty of conspiring against the flesh of our flesh and the blood of our blood. When we allow ourselves to make a habit of it; when we incorporate it into our daily routine and still have interaction with the brother/sister we are conspiring against only to never mention anything, well then we are allowing ourselves to be guilty of TREASON! Treason against the Almighty Latin King Queen Nation by means of conspiring against your kin.

How can one who allows themselves to be defined by the above be regarded as a true King/Queen?

You may be asking yourself, "Mission, where does technology play a role in all of this?" Well family, I ask that you take a moment to ask yourselves, "How many brothers/sisters who I have never physically met, do I communicate with over the internet? I am by no means saying that internet communication is wrong. On the contrary, through sites such as www.alkqn.org, I believe we can enjoy the benefits of creating relationships with brothers and sisters around the world. I do however; believe that we need to carefully scrutinize the communication that we receive. When the content of an e-mail or text message, or any kind of message for that matter, is filled with references to the demise of a black and gold sibling, we must assume the responsibility of directing that dissatisfied brother/sister back to the brother/sister he/she is dissatisfied with. If they choose not to heed the advice and follow the direction, then we must acknowledge the fact that they do not seek a resolution… they seek fame. They seek to have their name serve as the meaning behind the ALKQN. They are not recognizing that true Kings and Queens are servants of their communities and sincere to their Black and Gold family. There is no fame in a world that does not understand our goals. We were not chosen by the Father to be famous… we were chose to lead our community to greatness. This cannot be done if we cannot even lead each other to mean the Love that we speak of when we salute one another.

Those, whose nerves have been touched by my sentiments, must ask themselves, "Why?" Why is it that you feel offense by the expression of my opinion? Is it because my words form a shoe that is fitting too tightly? Is it because you fear your lies are losing their "power"? Perhaps I have made you look back at the time when you asked to stand in the light of the Almighty, and join our precious Nation, and you realize that all you said you were… you were only for that moment. The true you is one of disseat, dissatisfaction with your own life, no desire for true mobility, only desire for destruction. Perhaps you role your eyes, suck your teeth and disregard my sentiments; you say to yourself "Whatever, I know I am a real King. Mission doesn't know what he is talking about". To that, I ask where it is that my words became personal and why do you feel that I have not regarded you as a true King? If you feel the need to make a dozen phone calls, send a dozen e-mails, a dozen text messages to those who you "run with", I ask you; "Are you trying to put a battery in their back?", "Are you admitting to treason?" Those who simply nod in understanding knowing that their actions never exist with the intent of going against their own…especially those who have stood by their side as they started their journey into the light, will find it in their being to send an "Amor de Rey/Reina!", to a brother who chose to take a moment out to share his thoughts with his Black and Gold Family.

I close wishing you all the same blessings as when I opened. Though we strive for peace, may we always find the strength to keep our swords sharp and our shields shiny. It started with Love and has found eternal life through Love!! Behold!! Those who are sincere to themselves, their siblings, and their Nation, are TRUE ALMIGHTY LATIN KINGS AND QUEENS!!

Amor De Rey y Amor De Corona!!

THE TRUTH IS ACCESSIBLE

Each and every day our children are criminalized by a system that looks at the colors of their clothes with more attention than the content of their character. Our sons and daughters are judged by the music they listen to rather than appreciated for the ideas that they have.

The Almighty Latin King and Queen Nation is no stranger to the vicious attacks of a biased media and a judgmental society that would rather throw stones of hate at their neighbor than look at their own reflection and address the fallacies of their own existence. It is because of our experience and understanding that we take this time to draw attention to the trials and tribulations that we are all facing as a community. Poverty, drug abuse, police brutality, social injustice and the countless other social ills that plague us are not unique to us. We do not live in a bubble nor are we a species different than the rest of the bodies that form our local communities.

It is easy for one to label the ALKQN as a criminal organization based on the regular articles and stories on the internet. However, these articles do not make up the entire newspaper, nor do the stories serve as the corner stone of the internet. They are but tales of individuals, who have made individual decisions. Though at times their membership to the ALKQN is legitimate, more often than not, their true allegiance lies with criminal activity and therefore in defiance of our truth.

The Almighty Latin King and Queen Nation is NOT a criminal organization.

We are a Nation governed by a constitution that teaches us of righteousness and servant leadership. While a great number of our members find themselves incarcerated, they are in the company of Muslims, Christians... African Americans, Latinos, Asians, Caucasians... Fathers, Sons, Mothers, and Daughters... in summation, they find themselves in the company of every organization, denomination, ethnic group, and social title. To condemn the ALKQN because of the individual actions that a minority has made is to condemn all groups in the same manner. Is it not?

When the focus turns to our children, it is imperative that we, as a collective society, acknowledge the responsibility that we all have to raise them. We must not allow the internet to be the primary tool that our children learn about themselves, and the streets cannot become foster parents. We must never get so comfortable behind the screens of our computers and the screens of our cell phones, that we sacrifice the beauty of face to face communication.

We can only make the truth accessible to all who seek it... we cannot force anyone to understand.

Regardless of our affiliations and our alliances, we are all components of the same community and we owe it to ourselves and our children to work together.

Amor de Rey!

Amor de Reina!

Amor de Corona!

EVOLUTION IS LONG OVERDUE

Hello my brothers and sisters. I hope that when you all receive that you are all in the best of health and spirit. As for me, I continue to draw from the Brown Force of our people as well as the guidance of the Orishas to keep my head up. I thank the Almighty father for providing me with the strength to strive for a life that manifests Love, Honor, Obedience, Sacrifice and Righteousness as well as Respect, Honesty, Unity, Knowledge and Love. Amor De Rey!

Over the past 9 months I have had much time to reflect over the history of our precious Nation. Originating from the state of New York, I now reside in Arizona where I was blessed with the opportunity of exposing new brothers and sisters to the light therefore adding to the multitude of our family. In doing this I was able to think back to the goals our Nation has been trying to meet for decades.

Much time is spent talking about the need for the Nation to rise and receive the power and prestige that it deserves. However, in the very way that we talk of our precious Black and Gold we are feeding the very concept that holds it down. The Nation is not an entity outside of ourselves that we can speak of. The Nation is ourselves, it is an aspect of our being and can only progress once we have allowed ourselves to evolve and progress.

It pains me to see so many of our brothers and sisters stuck in idle while the world passes us by. We are - by nature - rulers of kingdoms and yet with all the bandannas, with all the beads, with all the yelling we have not truly begun to show pride in our Kingdoms for if we would, they would not be in the shambles they are in now. Our crowns, when illuminated by the light of Yahweh are blinding to the ignorant and so we should keep them in our hearts and minds where they are appreciated rather than wearing them around as clothing for the world to misunderstand.

Family, I implore you to realize the first 360 that needs to be attended is the one in yourself. Each and every one of us is an Almighty Latin King Queen Nation. Those who are dependent on us in our personal kingdoms are our first tribe. We cannot walk the streets of the concrete jungle claiming loyalty to the Crown and love for brothers and sisters we do not know simply because they say they are followers of the points, if we have not solidified a temple of true righteousness at home. We cannot teach our young Kings and Queens the ways of Kingism/Queenism if our own lives do not exemplify that curriculum. Every breathe we take should be done in a manner that is righteous or at very least, aspiring to be righteous.

This Nation that we speak of when separating it from ourselves is nothing more than a copout, an excuse used all too often to justify lack of personal accomplishments. The brother/sister that does not take the time to build his/her personal kingdom, wash the walls with Love, seal the windows with Honor, clothe its babies with obedience and feed its inhabitants with Sacrifice and Righteousness is the brother/sister that cannot stand toe to toe and proclaim his or her undying love and commitment to me. I say this because love of others is built on love of self and when one of our own shows a lacking in love of self by not making an effort to evolve and progress, then what they are proclaiming to me has no sincere emotional baking. They are doing nothing more than reciting words on paper.

Now don't get me wrong. I am not expecting all who seek the light to do so with an impeccable personal life. I am not asking that they be professionals in their field of interest and financially stable. I am however, expecting all to seek the light knowing that the world they knew yesterday was but a training ground for the world Yahweh is going to help them build tomorrow. I am asking that we seek to illuminate our personal and professional being with the same desire as we seek to illuminate our rep on the streets. Family, if all we have is the streets, then we are nothing more than what the rest of the world runs over to get to their destinations in life.

It is imperative that we stop finding the excuses for what is holding us back and take ownership of our future. No longer should we find contentment in reciting the same script that has been recited for decades in the 360. When the Almighty finds us together, we should be sharing our accomplishments and preparing each other for what is to come not dreaming and wondering if anything will ever be given to us.

My brothers and sisters, many have chosen to live in the light of Yahweh but their personal shadows make it impossible for them to ever achieve a level of Kingism/Queenism that has barely been mentioned in the lessons for it exists solely in yourself. This is the level of personal satisfaction and accomplishment. This is when the King/Queen looks at his/her children and says that they are true prince and princess because the foundation for their kingdom has been set and their thrown has been made. Now these shadows can be removed but you must be prepared to endure hardship and heartache for they are true battle wounds of evolution. While some may shake their heads at this I ask that other remember…. Many choose but few are chosen.

May the Almighty Father continue to guide you all. May your kingdoms be showered with blessings and its inhabitants receptive to and appreciating of those blessings. Let us remember that it began with Love and will find eternal existence because of Love. Though we strive for peace, the world has many battles that await us and so let us never keep are swords anything but sharp and our shields anything but shiny. Behold!! For the True Latin King/Queen knows self and enters the light with his/her natural crown understanding that his/her being is its own Nation. When pride and envy our put aside and we truly stand together as responsible and accountable Latinos, then all those Nations that live in the minds and hearts of our brothers and sisters come together to create what the world knows will one day rule…The Almighty Latin King Queen Nation. Amor De Rey!

EVOLUTION IS LONG OVERDUE II

Amor De Rey and Amor De Corona, my brothers and sisters. As always and forever, I hope that this finds you all in the best of health and spirit. As for me and mine, we continue to draw from the Brown Force of our Ancestors as well as the guidance of the Orishas to keep our heads up.

I send you all these sentiments with manifestations of Love, Honor, Obedience, Sacrifice and Righteousness as well as Respect, Honesty, Unity, Knowledge and Love.

Lately many of us have found ourselves on a familiar battlefield; A battlefield where both sides claim loyalty and devotion to the heavenly colors of Black and Gold. Again, both sides claim to be fighting for the best interest of the Nation, but it is only one of these sides that do not consider the Nation an entity separate from themselves. It is this side that rests its head at the side of the Almighty and it is this side who does not regard any battles won as a victory; for the brothers and sisters on this side understand that the war itself has the power to destroy us all.

I once wrote of the need for each and every brother/sister to evolve from a primitive state of being. I referred to this process as an internal one. Well now, I once again find myself asking my royal family to evolve. This time, I ask that the evolution take place in the way their mind prepares the agenda for the Nation as a whole.

For far too long brothers and sisters have awakened with an uncontrollable urge to lead the family. They have hungered for this power so feverishly that the foam falling from their mouths is proof that there desires are individualistic. And the way in which their agendas have been enforced is proof that they are ruling (or attempting to rule) subjects, not Kings and Queens…not brothers and sisters.

It is simply beyond me that after decades of existence there are still those who feel they hold all the answers. I have come across many of these brothers who have sat before their computer screens late at night, and manipulated the minds of brothers and sisters across this country the same way one might manipulate the pieces on a board game. They pride themselves on the number of brothers and sisters they "hold down", but rarely give that body the chance to be truly represented. The ideas, the goals, the dreams of all in that body are ignored and so in essence their royalty is ignored.

The time for speeches made by either self-proclaimed leadership or leadership whose crown comes in the form of pieces of paper that are never present when asked for, is long past. The world is much smaller than it was five years ago and our information is more accessible than it has ever been. Because of these changes, our methods of leadership must change. The time has long been present for each and every brother and sister to take ownership of their personal Kingdom. No longer can we afford to meet and stand toe-to-toe as an age old speech is recited by one who claims to represent us, but yet knows not even our name, let alone our own personal struggles.

By now, many are probably misinterpreting my words to mean that I am opposed to leadership and official structure. This is by no means the case. On the contrary, I agree with and support the need for structure and leadership. But leadership in a Nation of leaders needs to follow a different model. A model that understands the one at the head of the table is not better than those at the side; for he/she realizes that if there were no one at the sides of the table, then they would be alone.

Family, I ask that you once again look in the mirror and acknowledge your God given royalty. I ask that you wipe your eyes of the veil that has been sewn by servitude and see that before you assume a leadership role in the lives of anyone else, you must first assume and solidify leadership in your own world. Then, as your kingdom begins to shine with your own individual accomplishments, you can bring to the table fresh and constructive ideas that will then be recorded by the leadership you chose to represent you. The individual in leadership then has an obligation to distribute your ideas and accomplishments with the one concept that has a place no matter where you go on this planet….Love.

I close wishing you all the same blessings as when I opened. May the Almighty continue to guide and protect us all. Though we strive for peace, may we always find the strength to keep our swords sharp and our shields shiny. It started with Love and has found eternal life through Love. Behold!!

Amor De Rey and Amor De Corona!!

GANG VIOLENCE

What appears to be each and every day, the media is full of articles that highlight the horrible effects of gang violence, both in the United States and abroad. The words that have been strategically placed on newspapers and websites, paint pictures of teens covering the streets with their blood, families mourning, and community members who were oblivious to the situation, being dragged into urban war zones.

Each article seems to be more gruesome than the last and is always followed by an official statement from law enforcement that laws will be enforced and gang activity will not be tolerated.

The Almighty Latin King and Queen Nation continue to be one of the primary targets of law enforcement in the United States and abroad. The ALKQN has been labeled as a terrorist organization by senior level law enforcement agencies in the USA and efforts are made on a regular basis to dismantle the organization. However, when one takes the time to really look into the organization as a whole, one can clearly see that the purpose and principles of the organization are far from criminal and the majority of the membership is dedicated to lawful living and are actively involved in positive aspects of their community.

There is no doubt in my mind that as these words are read, heads are shaking in disagreement. "The Latin Kings are a bunch of criminals", may be the statement made by many. But ask yourself, "When was the last time the Almighty

Latin King and Queen Nation was in the news for killing a teenager, shooting an elderly woman as she came home from church, or chasing a woman out of her apartment complex?" These crimes are not simply examples created for the sake of making a point; they are articles that appeared in the press over the last week and a half involving gangs from all over the country.

Gang violence in this country, and abroad, is a serious problem and should be addressed. However, it is not a problem that can simply be addressed with new laws and more police. The issue of gang violence draws its strength from the ignorance and laziness of the community.

How long can we continue to read about 13 year olds being shot at 2am without asking the question of why a 13 year old was out alone at 2 am? Where was the family of this young teenager? Where was the embrace of love that kept this child from wondering the streets at an hour that invites others to act on their internal pain and manifest it into murder?

Can we not see how everything is connected?

Can we not see how the exorbitant costs of living in major cities has added to the decrease in time that parents are able to spend with their children, which in turn has inspired children to turn to the streets for parental guidance and support? Can we not see how the companies that allow "Scarface" t-shirts and other crime applauding paraphernalia to be created and sold in our communities are inspiring our children to live up to the tales of the individuals/groups that are being glamorized?

When do we, as the adults of our community, take responsibility for the situations that are going on in the streets of our community? When do we look in the mirror and recognize the role we play in the violence of gangs? What role you ask? The absent role that both inspired and allowed our children to turn to the streets and look for a way to make a name for themselves. When will we realize, accept, and address the fact that the companies that allow violent music to be produced, crime glorifying clothing to be manufactured, and emotionally numbing movies to be made are owned and operated by the same generation that is screaming at the existence of gang violence. Where do you think our children are getting their ideas from?

There are no 15 year old liquor store owners in any community.

There are no drug dealers that deal their poison for free… the community that wants them out is the same community that keeps them in business.

There are no adolescent record producers sitting in their office saying, “Hey, let’s make a song that teaches kids how to be gangster”.

The Almighty Latin King and Queen Nation asks the community to change the routine that has permitted our children to be lost and to create a routine of love and involvement. We encourage parents to talk with their children… not simply at their children. Learn about the daily activities of your children. Become involved in these activities and understand what motivates your children to want to do the things that they want to do. When your child comes home with a torn shirt, or a bruise, don't simply roll your eyes and label him/her a thug; ask your child what happened with sincere love and concern. Dress the wounds and embrace your child. Instead of cursing the streets that your child spends his/her time on, realize that they have come back home…. Home…the place where love and understanding should not only exist, but also be defined. Do more than simply pay the internet bill; sit with your child and ask them to show you what it is that they do while on the internet.

In no way is the ALKQN claiming to hold all the answers to the social ills that plague our community. Nor are we claiming that 100% of our membership is free of criminal activity. What we are doing, is acknowledging our place in the community and understanding that the streets of our neighborhoods are not exclusively owned by anyone, and so they belong to everyone. There are not enough corners for every group to think that they can live in complete seclusion. With that said, the ALKQN is formally requesting that the community get more involved in the issues that affect their neighborhoods, their communities, and their children. If you suspect your child of being involved with a gang or a street organization, speak with your child about it. Do not assume that screaming and yelling about an issue is going to have a positive effect.

Politicians and law enforcement agencies can make all of the laws they want. They can continue to allow their imaginations to run wild as they conjure up the penalties that criminals will face. However, none of that will put an end to the violence in our community. None of it will teach a parent how to be involved in their child's life. It is up to us to sit together and understand that we all breathe the same air, drink the same water, and walk the same streets.

HOW CAN YOU VERIFY A KING OR A QUEEN?

Amor de Rey y Corona, familia. As always and forever, I hope that when you read these words you and all in your kingdoms are in the best of health and spirit.

The question has been asked; "How can you tell who is real King?"

Many answers have been created for this specific question. I have seen members of our royal family become poets as they respond to this inquiry. I have seen others paint a picture with our literature as they respond, but when the written word was not enough, they inserted their own thoughts and opinions into the colors of the picture and tried to pass it off as facts.

The Nation has very clear guidelines on how to verify one's membership. There is no mystery that when one is presented with a brother / sister from another chapter, and the conversation extends any further than a personal: "Amor de Rey / Reina", the leadership of both chapters needs to be advised and both members need to be verified. Now, I know many of you are shaking your head in confusion at the possibility that your officials would need to be notified every time you have a conversation with someone, but read carefully what I have written. Let it be clearly understood that leadership need only get involved when the communication between two siblings graduates from a personal level to a level where Nation affairs are discussed.

It is no secret that each and every day hundreds of individuals chose to live on instant message programs and proclaim their undying devotion to the ALKQN. They write sentiments of loyalty and attempt to present themselves as experts of our literature and history. Many of these individuals are in their late teens or early twenties, have not been in the Nation very long, and have never traveled outside of their computer screen. Yet, it does not stop them from believing that they are all knowing. It does not stop them from ignoring the tools of the Nation and utilizing tools created by outsiders such as Myspace and Metro Flog.

The truth is that very little of the true history of the Nation is known outside of the United States. This is not to say that the brothers and sisters in the United States are better than anyone else, for they are absolutely not. It is simply to emphasize the fact that communication has not existed the way it should have between true Nation officials in the United States and other countries until now. As a result, many people seized the opportunity to teach their own version of our precious literature; a version that was convenient for them and promoted their own personal agenda. Today, the truth is accessible to all who seek it, but many continue to enjoy their ignorance and while they claim loyalty to the golden crown, they make every effort to keep their plastic copy on.

It has been said on various occasions that one of the reasons so much confusion exists is because those who originally taught us are no longer with us. I disagree with this statement. Again, the truth is accessible to all who desire to have it. Simply because we were taught a certain way, does not make it right. Many are running around in our Nation loyal to the teachings of the person who introduced them to the Nation. Imagine that… they are loyal to one person! With every breath they take they are going against the essence of the Nation; the essence of being loyal to the cause. "What is the cause?" you ask. The cause of us serving the communities that we live in and making them better. It doesn't matter how many friends you have on your website or how many messages you have showing, when you are doing nothing to improve your environment. Have we fallen so deep in our own egos that we have forgotten that our existence as a Nation came out of the needs that ALL Latinos have?

Confusion exists because although many sing the song of wanting to learn and wanting to grow, they only dance to the beat of ignorance. They follow the rhythm of fame and are controlled by the percussions of envy.

“Are you a Latin King or a Latin Queen?’ is a question that cannot be answered by sending someone a messenger invite or inviting them to view your metroflog!!

A true King/Queen does not hide behind the past. A true King/Queen works toward the creation of a better future and respects the protocols of our beloved Nation. A true King/Queen is not afraid to follow the policies and procedures of righteous leaders and understands that righteousness is not an empty term that we throw around like lose change in our pockets.

How can you tell if someone is a real King/Queen of the ALKQN? Have their credentials verified by your leadership.

If someone randomly appears, forces their opinion on you, speaks to you and not with you, and is reluctant to have their credentials verified, then they are probably not a King/Queen. If you continue to hang on their every word, then I would say that you are probably not a King/Queen either.

Remember, just because it is shiny does not mean it is gold… just because it is gold, does not mean it is a crown… just because it is a crown, does not mean it is royal… and just because it claims to be royal, does not mean it is a part of the Almighty Latin King and Queen Nation.

MESSAGE ABOUT KING BLOOD

Amor de Rey y Corona, familia. As always and forever, I hope that when you read these words you and all in your Kingdoms are in the best of health and spirit.

Today, as couples all over the world prepare to indulge in society's mandated embrace, many in our royal family recall a rainy Friday where the United States Court System buried one of our brothers alive.

February 14, 1997 was the day our brother King Blood was sentenced to life in prison plus an additional 45 years, all to be spent in solitary confinement. A sentence of this magnitude is virtually unprecedented and highlights the negative light that our community is seen under.

The pain was piercing as Blood said to Judge Martin, "I don't mind my mail to be monitored, but you are telling me, nobody can send money to me, nobody can care about me no more?"

The response was paralyzing when Judge Martin replied, "Exactly so".

Over the last 11 years, the events of that day, and the events leading to that day have been distorted, manipulated, and taken advantage of by many. What is even worse is that many of the individuals who have tried to gain from the circumstances surrounding hermano Blood, claim loyalty to the crown and the Almighty Latin King and Queen Nation.

In no way, shape, or form, was King Blood perfect… none of us are. We all have our vices and we all make mistakes. Blood's vision of growth for the ALKQN was an inspiring vision and many found a home on the path that led to the realization of this vision. Unfortunately, as many walked down this path, they turned their backs to the beginning of it and began to create their own road.

It is a sad reality that a common question exists in our Nation. This question is one that screams of ignorance and division… this question is, "Are you Blood Line or KMC?"

How can we allow ourselves to be manipulated by oppressive forces, and made to ask these questions of each other? What can be conceived as worse is that there are those who actually answer this question!

If you are a member of the Almighty Latin King and Queen Nation, then you are a representative of the Almighty Latin King and Queen Nation, which means that you run under the Almighty Latin King and Queen Nation…. Nothing more, nothing less.

If you find comfort and happiness in calling yourself a "Bloodline King/Queen" or a "KMC King/Queen", then it must be because you do not want to receive the light of the Almighty Father as an "Almighty Latin King and Queen Nation King/Queen".

How can anyone even begin to think that they are honoring the positive work that hermano Blood did, when they are feeding into the division that makes us weak. Blood was very clear every time he expressed himself, that there is only one constitution for the ALKQN and that it is to be adhered to at all times and without any excuses. This constitution is the KMC. The term "Blood Line" is not even a term that existed when hermano Blood was in the streets.

Today, and every day, I encourage you all to take a moment and acknowledge the sacrifices that many have made so that we can progress. I am not blind to the fact that not every sacrifice made by a member of our royal family was made selflessly for our family; but none the less, I am conscious of the fact that they are now on the digestive track of a beast we know as the Prison Industrial Complex.

We are already aware that many choose and few are chosen.... The new question is what are you choosing to be and who are you choosing to belong to?

If you find pleasure in futile fame... if you find satisfaction in spewing sarcastic stories... if you find love in lying.... Then you will never find the true Almighty Latin King and Queen Nation.

NEW STRUCTURE = NO STRUCTURE

Amor De Rey and Amor De Corona, my brothers and sisters. As always, I hope that when you receive this, you are all in the best of health and spirit. As for me and mine, we continue to draw from the Brown Force of our Ancestors as well as the guidance of the Orishas to keep our heads up.

Since my emergence into the light, I have always searched for new ways for our Black and Gold family to collectively evolve and progress. I learned fairly quickly, that the Nation is not an entity outside of ourselves and we cannot blame it for creating a violent reputation or severing the ties with the very community we seek to uplift. It was easy to lose myself in the drama of day to day life and end the night with the ever popular statement of, "The Nation is stressing me". It wasn't until recently that I fully realized that the "Nation" was not really, nor could it ever stress me. I was stressing myself by allowing a few individuals to have the power over me to alter my mood.

Time went on and it seemed that no matter how great our accomplishments or how big a step we took in the right direction, we always ended up in the same place. We were fighting each other, we were leery of one another, and we had reservations of many whom we called brother and sister and we were ultimately losing time. The brothers and sisters we came to regard as those in the structure were constantly being replaced and rearranged. The general body had little voice if any, and the Nation as the outside world began to know it was represented by the faces of a select few.

When I first came to Arizona, I came into contact with people who had never heard of the Almighty Latin King and Queen Nation. It was a culture shock to me as I am originally from New York City and there is no escaping our reputation there. I immediately saw the opportunity to build a Kingdom whose foundation was free of stories from the past, promised positions, animosity and turmoil. I felt as if Arizona could be another part of the planet (Cuba was the first for me), where the Nation could be born in the minds of new brothers and sisters as opposed to brothers and sisters looking to be born again into the Nation. With new found excitement and drive, I began on the road known to all who bring the light to a dark place and followed an unofficial routine that has existed for decades.

Again time went on and before long, the foundation was built. Before me stood strong, proud and inspired Lions who were anxious to roar with the masses. Unfortunately, our time for utopian celebration was cut short.

As is the case with every structure that has ever existed, the duty of guiding the people is often fulfilled by governing the people. While the entire structure (myself included) was voted in after the body was big enough to do so; there inevitably came times when the voters and the voted clashed. I began to see a scenario that was all too familiar for me. Despite all of our efforts to keep the tone of the chapter leveled, and despite our emphasizing that no one was better than or worth more than the other, a hierarchy was developing. Those elected into leadership started to make the mistake of carrying the decades of drama this Nation has had, on their shoulders. Collectively we were trying to bring our precious Nation to the next level, but it was as if we were being weighed down by an invisible force.

The last weekend in February I had the opportunity to sit with a brother who is very dear to me. He was with me when I searched for the light and warned me of the consequences that I would have to face if I continued my search. He always regarded me as one of his sons and I know now that it wasn't that he didn't want me to get down, it was that he didn't want me to be held down. At any rate, the Almighty allowed for our meeting after years of separation and the words that were spoken cleared my mind in such a way that I was able to see what we were doing wrong back home.

With a strong embrace, I thanked the brother for expressing himself so sincerely that it allowed me to hear what my guardian spirits had been telling me for years, but I chose to ignore.

On March 7, 2004, the Arizona State Almighty Latin King and Queen Nation held a meeting. The meeting was held in the same location as the crownings are held. It was at this meeting that I addressed the body as a member of the body; No position, no traditional formalities, just a brother expressing himself. I explained that my mind was racing with new thoughts that had been thought of in new ways. I expressed my Love and Pride with the body and assured them that although I fathered the majority of them into our Nation, no one was better than the brother or sister that stood beside them. I asked security to come from their posts and sit with us as no one brother's/sister's life was more valuable than the next. I explained that we all had an obligation to ourselves and each other…. in that order. No longer could we convince ourselves that our willingness to die for one another superseded all things. We needed to understand that without something to live for, without a solid personal foundation, we are not Almighty Kings and Queens. Without a strong sense of worth and purpose, we are nothing more than members of a clique mastering the art of imagery. Our bodies, draped in the colors of royalty, become an image of brotherhood and sisterhood. We are quick to profess our willingness to die for one another but hesitate when asked to truly live for something.

I went on to say that to love this Nation is to Love yourself, and to see this Nation succeed is to succeed yourself. I explained that my opinion – not necessarily a fact – is that once we achieve knowledge of self, then we are inevitably royal. Our Crowns should never be up for discussion. The literature that serves as the foundation of this Nation should be a mirror that forces each King and Queen to look at themselves. The lessons are not prepared to walk us through the world we live in today; A world where the community has been sacrificed so that the planet can be made smaller. A world where young men and women have friends in other countries that they communicate with via the internet, but they do not even know their neighbor's name.

The discussion of uniting Latinos all over the planet is one that has existed for far too long. It is one that while inspiring the newly involved, also serves as sign of defeat for the veteran activists. What progress have we really made?

If we were to gather each and every Latin King and Latin Queen from all over the world, get them all to be on the same page and function as a true family, would this make the world a better place? Can we guarantee that we will actually make a difference or will we still be stuck on who is holding what? Will the voice of the brother/sister with five months in be as heard and respected as the brother/sister with five years? What if the answer to these questions is in fact yes? What about the rest of the community? What about those who are not truly Black and Gold, but pick up a flag with the hope that someone's gangsta was represented so "strongly" that no one will question theirs?

Family, as is the case with all the sentiments I share, I implore you not to misunderstand me. I am not overlooking the accomplishments that we have made. I am not overlooking our progress. What I am saying is that we are running around in circles. Our accomplishments – if truly analyzed – can be attributed to the existence of specific individuals. We are not functioning as a single unit because we are not made to be a single unit. You cannot rise each day thinking that you are just another Latin King/Queen in the Nation. You must rise and exist each day knowing that you are the sheer essence of the Almighty Latin King and Queen Nation. When you see another brother/sister, acknowledge them for the Nation that they are and find comfort that our foundations are the same, but our progress is different. What we are members of, is the Latino community. A community that suffers from the ills of drugs, violence and corruption. If all we focus on is how to make the 360 bigger, how are we truly improving our community? Are we to believe that all who are scouted return to the circle out of Love? How many of us are guilty for preaching that as natural Kings and Queens we have the right to make decisions and to choose for ourselves? Is this not a God given right? When did the Almighty leave it up to our structure to decide what choices are correct or not? I tell all whom I meet, I am by your side because I dedicate my life to the upliftment of our people. You are my brother/sister because you are Latino and our history is one of struggle. You are welcome into my Kingdom because you are sincere and strive to be righteous. You are King/Queen because our ancestors where royalty. You are Black and Gold because you feel the roar of the Lion in your heart and you wish to do more than the average person.

Family, on March 7, 2004, the Arizona State Almighty Latin King and Queen Nation held a vote. By unanimous decision, we did away with all positions. We acknowledge the fact that we can only truly be responsible for our own actions and we can no longer afford to be sucked into the mindset that convinces us that we have dominion over anyone else's life. Understanding that not all of our family will agree with our move, we ask that all realize that to stand by each other's side, Love and Respect are needed… not stone. The primary position we all hold is that of King/Queen and that is all that is needed to build a relationship.

Our focus is to progress as individuals and reach a level where we will truly be able to help our people and our community. No longer are we content with discussions about what could be or what should be. There is only room to discuss what is being done. A representative has been elected to establish and maintain communication with the family all over the world, and at any time, the body can elect to have that representative changed.

Now more than ever, the pride of the Crown is felt by our body. Now more than ever we can appreciate the brilliance of the Gold and understand the solace of the Black. We understand that our Nation has a history, and we emphasize the teaching of it…not its repetition.

I close wishing you the same blessings as when I opened. May the Almighty continue to guide and protect you all and all in your Kingdoms. Though we strive for peace, may we always find the strength to keep our swords sharp and our shields shiny. Behold!!

Amor De Rey and Amor De Corona!!

WAKE UP

Amor de Rey y Corona, familia. As always and forever, I hope that when you read these words you all and all in your Kingdoms are in the best of health and spirit.

I write these words lost in reflection on the actions that so many take in the name of love and loyalty to the Almighty Latin King and Queen Nation. I reflect on the inconsistencies that have come to define the masses who claim to represent the strength and beauty of Black and Gold, but in reality simply like the color combination and think that adorning themselves will make them superior.

I think of miserable individuals who allow themselves to become drunk with envy and remove their crowns of righteousness for hats of envy and disgust. These are the individuals who exist with opinions of individuals and situations that they do not know personally and do not understand. They present their own beliefs as facts because if they do not, they then run the risk of acknowledging their own invalidity. These individuals claim to roar as lions, but in reality are simply whimpering as hyenas when they leave threatening messages on voicemails of those who are truly dedicated to the cause of our progression, disrespect the virtue of our beautiful queens, disregard the decisions of our leadership engaging in such activities as presenting themselves to the public as royalty when they know without doubt that the gates of the ALKQN have closed behind them and they have been expelled. Has "Amor de Rey" become a popular lyric that is sang to pass the time, or does it remain the cry of the chosen to remind that the Nation was before them and will be after them?

One need only spend a few minutes on the internet to see a world of grey and yellow that many try to present as a world of Black and Gold.

Commitment to our dear Nation requires more than taking a dozen pictures of yourself and posting them on a social website and sitting behind a computer all day logged into a messenger program where you write about the trials and tribulations of your streets. How can anyone speak, with any kind of authority, about the social issues that affect their community if their community has become the people sitting around them and renting time on the computer in the cyber café?

Perhaps at some point the message was sent out that the ALKQN was a social club where fame and fortunate could be obtained. If that was the case, on behalf of the true senior leadership, allow me the opportunity to apologize.

The Almighty Latin King and Queen Nation is not a social club, nor is it the personal playground of anyone individual who claims to be above anyone else. The Almighty Latin King and Queen Nation is an organization of brotherhood, sacrifice, commitment, love, intelligence, and responsibility.

Recently I had the opportunity to sit with a brother who recently relocated to the United States from another country. As I listened to him explain to me what he believed the culture of the Nation was it was clear to me that many continue to occupy their time by creating rules and regulations that only make sense to them. They become consumed by what they consider to be the remedies to their local problems, but ignore (almost completely), the one true and only constitution… the KMC. I am not saying that it is not advantageous or allowed for chapters to create their own rules and regulations (that do not conflict with the constitution), because it is. However, it is simply ignorant and not a show of royalty to build on a foundation that is not solid. How can a chapter create rules and regulations that uphold their own local "culture" if the true culture of the ALKQN is not first known, understood, respected, and abided by all in the chapter? The answer is, "they can't".

My dear brothers and sisters, “Wake Up!”

Wake up and understand that being a King/Queen in the ALKQN is not a part-time duty. “Everybody makes mistakes” is not a valid excuse for anyone to continually disrespect our constitution, our laws, our protocol… our purpose. The existence of our beloved Nation comes through the blood, sweat, and tears of countless men and women who are turning over in their graves at the fact that there are individuals who claim that they are true to the ALKQN but do everything in defiance of the constitution. How are you respecting the sacrifices of true brothers and sisters when you use our greeting in vain and extend your crown to those who have been expelled? Why is it that so many think that because they are friends with someone that their membership serves as valid for the two of them? Do you not realize that you are not recognized by the Nation Eye? Do you not understand that in the comfort of your own home, you can be an entire Kingdom… however, when you step foot into the real concrete jungle of life, you are nothing more than a spoiled snack for true lions. Many speak of the Brown Force that guides us… however; very few allow themselves to be guided. In case there was any doubt, allow me the opportunity to remind everyone that complaining, gossiping, conspiring, and attempting to manipulate the literature and rules to fit your own personal agenda is not the behavior of a King/Queen of the ALKQN. It is, however, the behavior of the oppressive forces that sit and laugh at the comic relief we provide when we turn on each other.

My dear brothers and sisters, “Wake Up!”

Wake up and realize the arsenal that is created when you have sincere understanding. Realize that the pulse of the ALKQN comes from the body of the ALKQN… a body that is made by the people. As an indispensable organ, you have an obligation to beat Love, Honor, Obedience, Sacrifice, and Righteousness.

www.ingramcontent.com/pod-product-compliance
Ingram Content Group UK Ltd.
Pitfield, Milton Keynes, MK11 3LW, UK
UKHW041916190726
13854UKWH00003B/1269

9 781105 645488